I0815761

DISCOVERING THE UNITED STATES

Oklahoma

BY BARBARA LOWELL

Kids Core

An Imprint of Abdo Publishing
abdobooks.com

abdobooks.com

Printed in China.
052024
092024

Cover Photo: Kit Leong/Shutterstock Images
Interior Photos: Shutterstock Images, 4–5, 14; William Leaman/Alamy, 7 (top left); A. LaRue/Alamy, 7 (top right); JHVE Photo/Shutterstock Images, 7 (bottom left); O. S. Fisher/Shutterstock Images, 7 (bottom right); Gabbro/Alamy, 8; Heeb Christian/Prisma by Dukas Presseagentur GmbH/Alamy, 10–11; Robin Rudd/Chattanooga Times Free Press/AP Images, 13; Kit Leong/Shutterstock Images, 21, 25; Sue Ogrocki/AP Images, 16, 28 (bottom); Sean Pavone/Shutterstock Images, 18–19; John Elk/The Image Bank/Getty Images, 22; Lee Rentz/Alamy, 26; Red Line Editorial, 28 (top left), 29 (top); Michael Woods/Alamy, 28 (top right); iStockphoto, 29 (bottom)

Editor: Christa Kelly
Series Designer: Katharine Hale

Library of Congress Control Number: 2023949366

Publisher's Cataloging-in-Publication Data

Names: Lowell, Barbara, author.
Title: Oklahoma / by Barbara Lowell
Description: Minneapolis, Minnesota: Abdo Publishing, 2025 | Series: Discovering the United States | Includes online resources and index.
Identifiers: ISBN 9781098294069 (lib. bdg.) | ISBN 9798384913337 (ebook)
Subjects: LCSH: U.S. states--Juvenile literature. | Oklahoma--History--Juvenile literature. | Southwestern States--Juvenile literature. | Physical geography--United States--Juvenile literature.
Classification: DDC 973--dc23

All population data taken from:
"Estimates of Population by Sex, Race, and Hispanic Origin: April 1, 2020 to July 1, 2022." *US Census Bureau, Population Division*, June 2023, census.gov.

CONTENTS

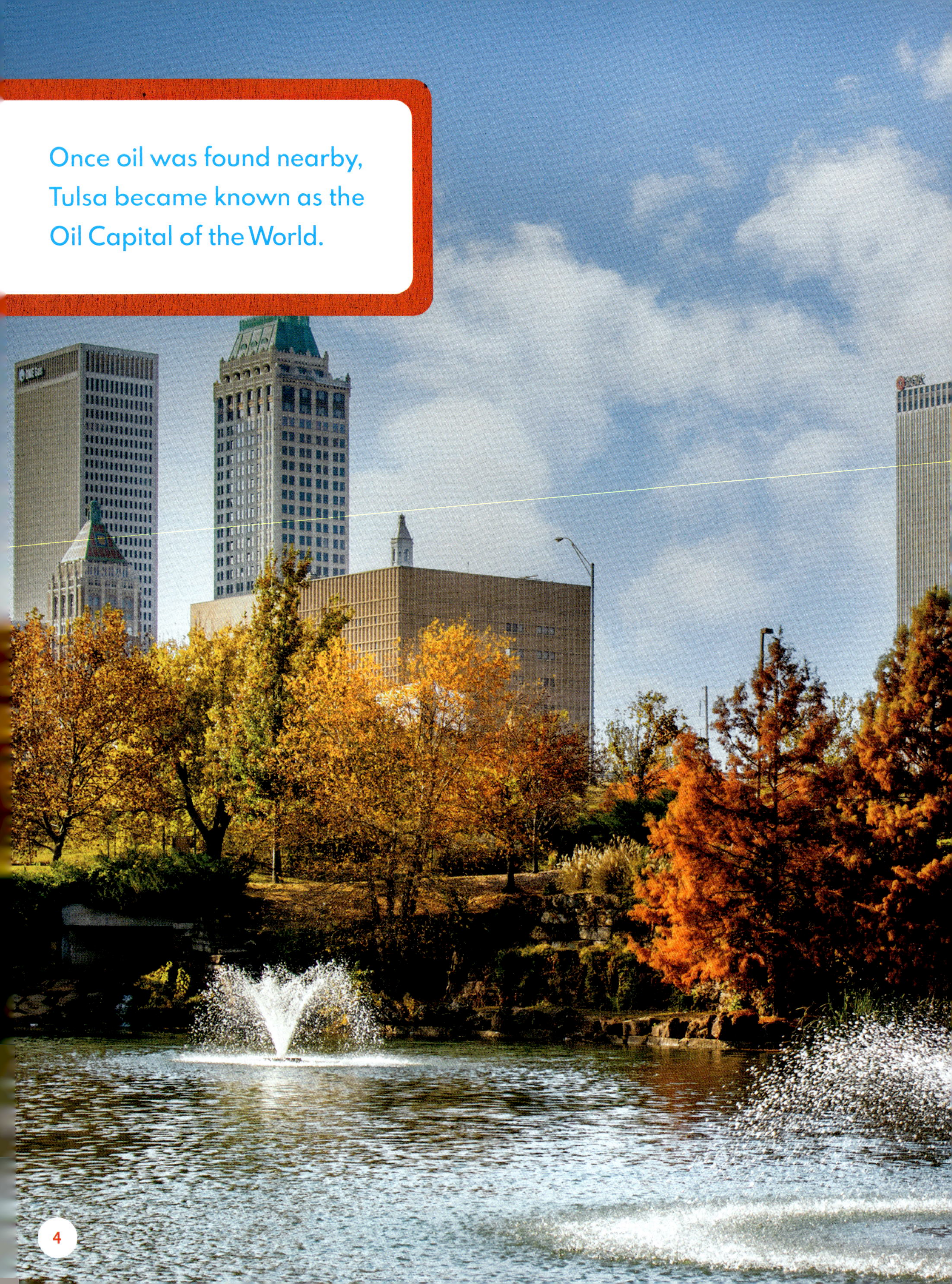

Once oil was found nearby, Tulsa became known as the Oil Capital of the World.

CHAPTER 1

Oil in Oklahoma

In 1901, an oil driller named Robert Galbreath arrived at Ida E. Glenn's farm. Glenn thought her land might have oil. Oil is valuable. It can be used to make fuels such as gas.

Galbreath was there to find out if there was oil underground.

He drilled down more than 1,400 feet (427 m). There was no oil. He was about to give up. Then, he heard a roar. The ground shook, and oil shot into the sky. Today, the oil-rich land provides thousands of jobs for the people of Oklahoma.

Oklahoma's Land

Oklahoma is in a region of the United States called the South. The state is bordered by Kansas and Colorado to the north.

Tornadoes

The western half of Oklahoma sits in Tornado Alley. This region of the United States gets frequent tornadoes. Since 1950, Oklahoma has averaged 57 tornadoes a year.

Oklahoma Facts

DATE OF STATEHOOD
November 16, 1907

CAPITAL
Oklahoma City

POPULATION
4,019,800

AREA
69,899 square miles
(181,038 sq km)

STATE BIRD

Scissor-tailed flycatcher

STATE TREE

Redbud

STATE FLOWER

Oklahoma rose

STATE MAMMAL

American bison

Each US state has a different population, size, and capital city. States also have state symbols.

Arkansas and Missouri lie to the east. New Mexico borders Oklahoma's **panhandle** to the west. Texas lies to the south, separated from Oklahoma by the Red River.

Many animals live in Oklahoma's Ouachita Mountains, including bobwhite quail.

The Wichita Mountains are in southwestern Oklahoma. The Ouachita Mountains stretch across southeastern Oklahoma. The state has large regions filled with grass-covered hills and prairies. Prairies are large grasslands.

Bluestem grass grows in the eastern and central regions. Buffalo grass is common in the west.

Oklahoma also has many forests. Oak and hickory trees are scattered throughout the state. Pine forests are found in southeastern Oklahoma.

Oklahoma has hot summers, mild falls, and cold winters. The spring season is known for its dangerous weather. Severe spring storms bring high winds, hail, floods, and tornadoes.

Further Evidence

Visit the website below. Does it give any new information about Oklahoma that wasn't in Chapter One?

Animals of Oklahoma

abdocorelibrary.com/discovering-oklahoma

The Comanche people are known as the Lords of the Plains.

CHAPTER 2

The People of Oklahoma

American Indians have lived in Oklahoma for 30,000 years. They formed distinct nations. These included the Caddo, Quapaw, and Comanche. Other nations hunted in the region.

There are 39 American Indian nations in Oklahoma today.

Some originally lived in the eastern part of the United States. These include the Cherokee and Chickasaw.

In the 1830s, the US government forced Indian nations to leave their homes and move west. This journey is known as the Trail of Tears. The government called the land they were resettled in Indian **Territory**. In the late 1800s, Indian Territory became known as Oklahoma. In 1907, Oklahoma became the forty-sixth state.

Oklahoma Today

Today, Oklahoma has the second-highest percentage of American Indians in the country. American Indians make up 9.5 percent of people in the state. About 63 percent of people

Every year, members of the Cherokee Nation remember their ancestors by biking 950 miles (1,500 km) along the Trail of Tears.

in Oklahoma are white, and 12 percent are Hispanic or Latino. Almost 8 percent are Black. Nearly 3 percent are Asian.

Many people in Oklahoma are farmers. Oklahoma is among the country's top producers of beef. Others raise chickens and pigs for meat.

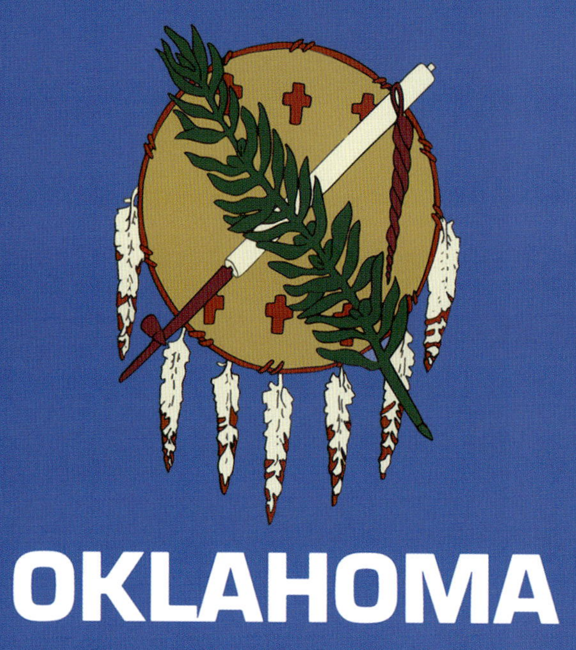

Oklahoma's state flag features a shield, an olive branch, and an American Indian pipe called a *calumet.*

Wheat is a common crop. A lot of Oklahoma's wheat is used to make bread.

Energy production is another important **industry** in Oklahoma. Many people have jobs producing and transporting **natural gas** and oil. Oklahoma is the third-biggest natural gas producer in the country.

Culture

Food is an important part of Oklahoma's culture. Oklahoma is known for its barbecue and fry bread. People also make fried catfish.

Sports are also a big part of Oklahoma's culture. College football is the most popular sport in Oklahoma. The state has two nationally known college football teams. They are the Oklahoma Sooners and the Oklahoma State Cowboys. Other people in Oklahoma enjoy attending **rodeos**.

Noodling

Some people in Oklahoma enjoy noodling. When noodling, people try to catch a flathead catfish with their bare hands. These fish can weigh up to 50 pounds (20 kg).

The Roy Leblanc Okmulgee Invitational Rodeo is one of the longest-running rodeos in Oklahoma.

Powwows are also important to many people in Oklahoma. During powwows, members of American Indian nations come together to celebrate their heritage. They speak their native languages and enjoy traditional foods. They sing and dance.

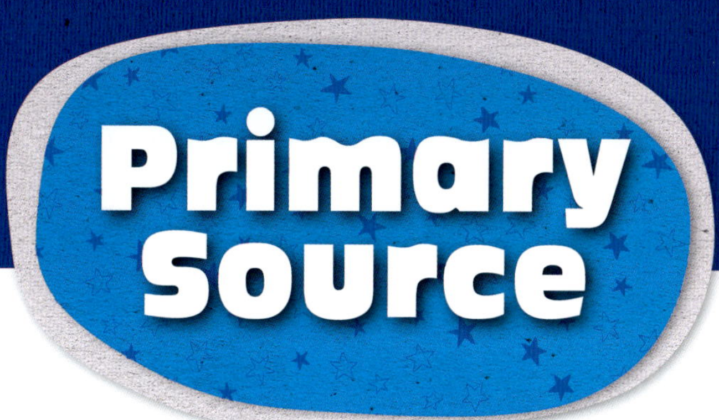

In 1836, Cherokee Nation chief John Ross wrote to Congress. He objected to the removal of the Cherokee people from their native lands. He said:

> We are deprived of membership in the human family! We have neither land nor home, nor resting place that can be called our own.

Source: "Cherokee Letter Protesting the Treaty of New Echota," *PBS*, n.d., pbs.org. Accessed 31 Oct. 2023.

What's the Big Idea?

Read this quote carefully. What is its main idea? Explain how the main idea is supported by details.

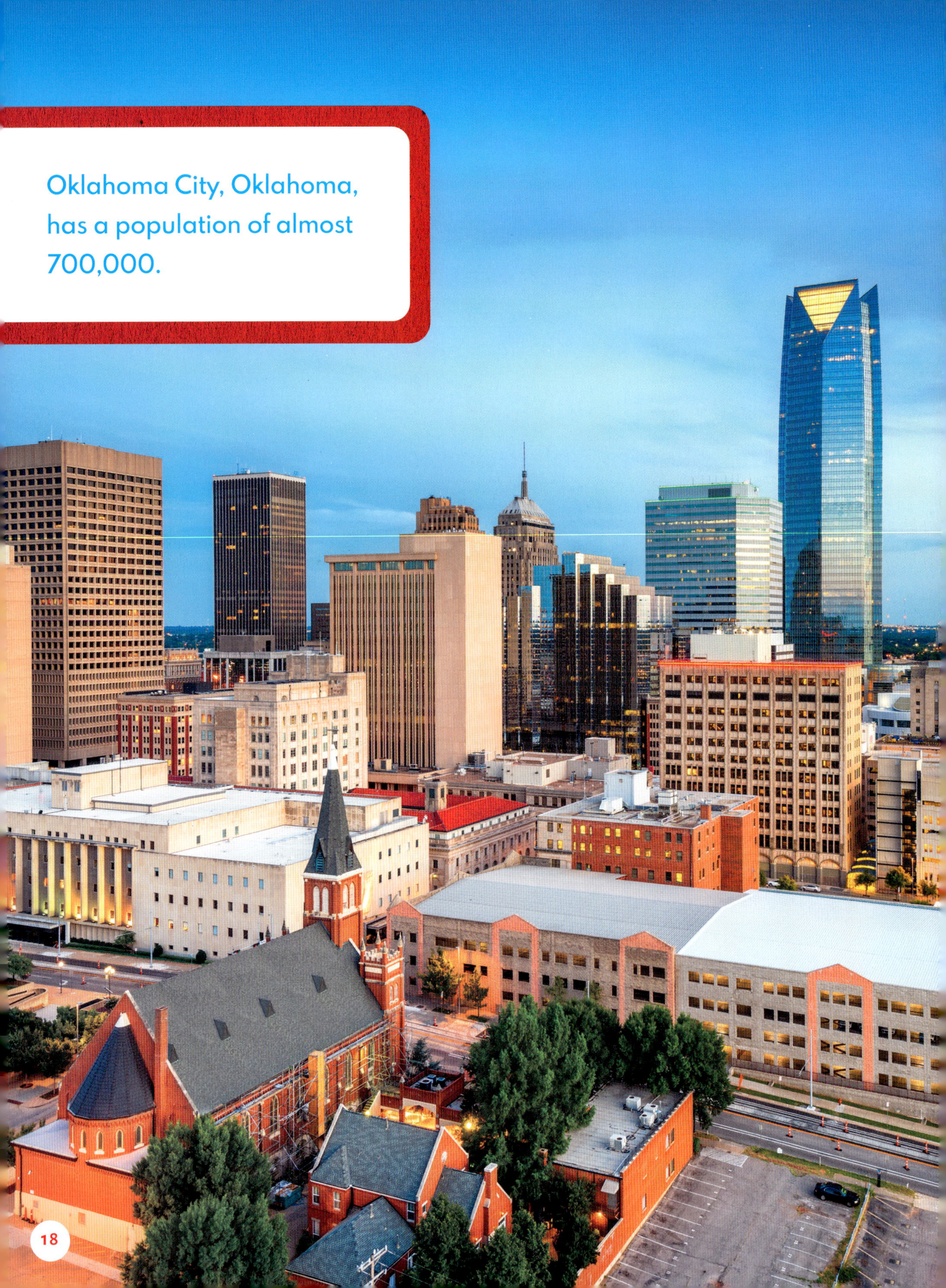

Oklahoma City, Oklahoma, has a population of almost 700,000.

CHAPTER 3

Places in Oklahoma

Oklahoma City is the capital of Oklahoma. It is also the state's largest city. The city is home to the Oklahoma City Zoo.

Visitors to Oklahoma City can see the beautiful Myriad Botanical Gardens. The gardens stretch across 15 acres (6 ha).

Inside the gardens are an ice rink, a splash pad, and a carousel. The gardens also host art exhibits. Almost 1 million people visit the gardens every year.

Tulsa is Oklahoma's second-largest city. It has several art museums. These include the Philbrook Museum and the Gilcrease Museum. Both museums have large collections of American Indian art.

Tulsa is also the site of Greenwood, a large Black community that was destroyed by a mob of white people in 1921. The community struggled to rebuild. The Greenwood Rising History Center teaches people about the tragedy. The museum has audio recordings of survivors sharing their stories.

The Myriad Botanical Gardens opened in 1988.

Black Mesa is the highest point in Oklahoma.

Parks and Nature

Oklahoma has 38 state parks. One of its most popular is Black Mesa State Park. The park is in Oklahoma's panhandle. It is home to black bears, mountain lions, bobcats, antelope, and bighorn sheep.

Robbers Cave State Park is another popular park. It is in eastern Oklahoma. The park covers 8,000 acres (3,000 ha) of land.

Dinosaur Tracks

In the 1980s, dinosaur tracks were found near Black Mesa State Park. The 47 **fossilized** tracks were from a large dinosaur that roamed the land millions of years ago. Scientists believe the dinosaur walked on two legs and ate meat. The dinosaur may have been a *Tyrannosaurus rex*.

One of the caves in the park is famous for being the hideout of Belle Starr. She was an outlaw during the late 1800s.

Chickasaw National Recreation Area is a popular tourist destination. The Chickasaw Nation used to own the land. The park is located in Sulphur, a town in southern Oklahoma. Tourists visit the park to swim, hike, and boat.

Landmarks

Oklahoma has many landmarks. Some honor the state's American Indians. Washita Battlefield National Historic Site is in western Oklahoma. It honors members of the Cheyenne nation who died in an 1868 US military attack. People can learn about the site's history at the visitor center.

The Chickasaw National Recreation Area covers 9,899 acres (4,006 ha).

The Cherokee National History Museum is another important landmark. The museum is in Tahlequah in eastern Oklahoma. It teaches visitors about the history and culture of the Cherokee people.

Sod houses were made of bricks of dirt, grass, and roots.

People in Aline in Northern Oklahoma can visit the Sod House Museum. It protects the last remaining sod house in Oklahoma. The home was built by Oklahoma **settlers** in 1894. They lived in the house until 1909. Visitors can walk through the house and learn about what life was like for the settlers.

Oklahoma is an exciting place to live and work. People can visit the state to watch sports and see beautiful natural sites. Whether a person likes hiking, learning about history, or catching catfish, there's plenty to do in Oklahoma.

Explore Online

Visit the website below. Does it give new information about settlers that was not in Chapter Three?

Sod House Museum

abdocorelibrary.com/discovering-oklahoma

State Map

KEY

Capital
Park
City or town
Point of interest

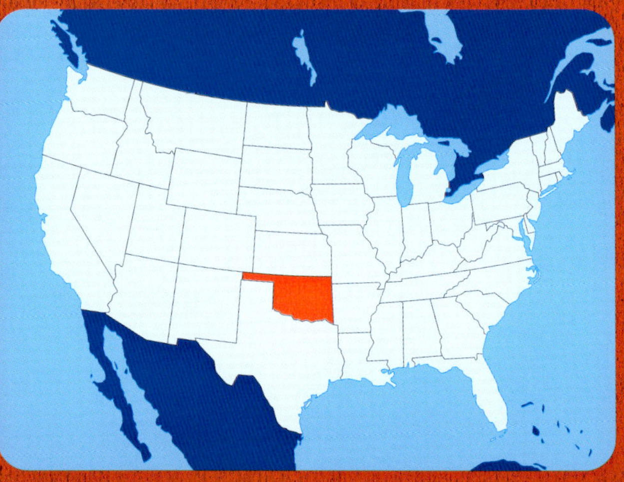

Oklahoma City Zoo

Robber's Cave State Park

Oklahoma: The Sooner State

Colorado
Kansas
Missouri
Arkansas
New Mexico
Texas
Black Mesa State Park and Nature Preserve
Arkansas River
Sod House Museum
Tulsa
Grand Lake o' the Cherokees
Oklahoma City
Washita Battlefield
Spiro Mounds Archaeological Center
Wichita Mountains Wildlife Refuge
OUACHITA MOUNTAINS
Norman
Eufaula Lake
WICHITA MOUNTAINS
Lawton
Robbers Cave State Park
Red River
Chickasaw National Recreation Area
Lake Texoma
N
W
E
S

Wichita Mountains Wildlife Refuge

Glossary

fossilized
preserved from a very long time ago, such as imprints in stone

industry
a group of businesses that serve similar purposes

natural gas
a mix of gases found underground that can be used as fuel

panhandle
an area of land that, on a map, is narrow like the handle of a frying pan

rodeos
events where people ride, capture, and wrestle cows

settlers
people who moved to a new area

territory
a particular area of land that belongs to and is governed by a country

Online Resources

To learn more about Oklahoma, visit our free resource websites below.

Visit **abdocorelibrary.com** or scan this QR code for free Common Core resources for teachers and students, including vetted activities, multimedia, and booklinks, for deeper subject comprehension.

Visit **abdobooklinks.com** or scan this QR code for free additional online weblinks for further learning. These links are routinely monitored and updated to provide the most current information available.

Learn More

Bird, F. A. *Cherokee*. Abdo, 2022.

Buckley, Patricia Morris. *The First Woman Cherokee Chief: Wilma Pearl Mankiller*. Penguin Random House, 2023.

Murray, Julie. *Oklahoma*. Abdo, 2020.

Index

About the Author

Barbara Lowell is an award-winning author of nonfiction picture books, early readers, and educational chapter books. She lives in Broken Arrow, Oklahoma.